My First Tutu

From the time I was about three years old, I loved cutting out ballet pictures and coloring in my ballet coloring book and telling my mother I wanted to do that. But all the ballet studios told my mother I was too young and would lose interest if she enrolled me.

When I was five, a neighbor gave me a pink tutu to wear as a Halloween costume. In case my mother didn't get the idea that I wanted to take ballet, I started wearing my tutu around the house. Finally, she got the hint and started me in a creative dance class. But I did not really like modern dance.

I wanted to dance on my toes.

Darci doing what she does best in The Magic Flute.

Ballerina

My Story
by Darci Kistler

with Alicia Kistler

A Byron Preiss Book

A MINSTREL BOOK

PUBLISHED BY POCKET BOOKS

New York   London   Toronto   Sydney   Tokyo

Special thanks to Judy Gitenstein for her work on the manuscript. Additional thanks to Pat MacDonald and Ruth Ashby.

Book Design by Alex Jay/Studio J
Typesetting by Books International
Associate Editor: Kathy Huck
Editorial Assistant: Vicky Rauhofer

A MINSTREL PAPERBACK ORIGINAL

A Minstrel Book published by
POCKET BOOKS, a division of Simon & Schuster Inc.
1230 Avenue of the Americas, New York, NY 10020

ISBN: 0-671-64437-8

First Minstrel Books printing December 1993

10 9 8 7 6 5 4 3 2 1

A MINSTREL BOOK and colophon are registered trademarks of Simon & Schuster Inc.

Printed in U.S.A.

INTRODUCTION

This book tells you all about what it's like to be a ballerina. I am a ballerina with the New York City Ballet, the largest ballet company in the United States. People ask me how I decided to become a ballerina. I tell them I've never imagined being anything else. Ever since I can remember I've wanted to dance on pointe, on the tips of my toes, in special beautiful handmade shoes, to the most beautiful music in the world. I've known what I wanted to do since I was eight years old.

In many ways, I was just like other kids growing up. I had lots of girlfriends in elementary school and junior high, and we would try on makeup and talk about boys. But when the bell rang, I knew I couldn't wait to get to ballet class.

As a child, I loved fairy tales. I always thought they were real because they had all the essential elements of life: good and evil, joy and sorrow, love and loss, life and death. Fairy tales transported me to a different age, a different time. My favorites were *Swan Lake, Rapunzel,* and *Cinderella*. When I read *The Sleeping Beauty* as a little girl, I had no idea that one day I would be dancing my dream role, Princess Aurora.

You don't have to want to be a dancer to enjoy this book. You don't have to know anything about ballet or dance of any kind. That's because this book is about figuring out what you want to do and working hard toward your goal. It's a book about having a dream and making that dream come true. As you read my story I hope that you will also think about the dreams you want to come true for you.

—Darci Kistler

PROLOGUE

It was the evening of December 2, 1989. I stood backstage at the John F. Kennedy Center for the Performing Arts, in Washington, D.C. I was about to perform a scene from the ballet *Swan Lake* for the 1989 Kennedy Center Honors as a tribute to Madame Alexandra Danilova, who had been one of my teachers at the School of American Ballet. Now she was one of five people being presented with a Lifetime Achievement Award.

This was an extremely important and emotional evening for me. Mme Danilova first performed this role in the 1920s, when she was a young dancer. She passed the knowledge of the role on to me years later when she helped me to prepare for one of my most important student performances. I wanted my dancing that evening to be a thank-you for her guidance. I wanted it to be perfect.

As I waited for my cue, I checked my headpiece to make sure it was secure. I straightened my costume and bent down to adjust the ribbons on my toe shoes. I heard my music begin and I floated out onstage, transformed from a person to a swan. As I danced, I lost all awareness of the moment. I became part of Tchaikovsky's beautiful music. And then I heard the audience clapping and it was time for me and my partner to take our bows.

I thought back to the first time I had danced on this stage, nine years earlier, on October 8, 1980, when I had just been made a member of the New York City Ballet. I thought about my fairy-tale career. At fourteen I had gone to New York to study at the School of American Ballet. Two years later, I was selected by the director of the New York City Ballet, Mr. George Balanchine, to join the company. I was given my first major role at age sixteen.

I thought of all the long, hard work it took me to get to this point. Of how I overcame not just one but two injuries. I had made a comeback to dance a tribute to someone who had passed on to me a great tradition—of ballet, of beauty. It was one of the happiest moments of my life.

CHAPTER 1

SOME BASIC INFORMATION ABOUT BALLET

There are many different kinds of dance: modern, folk, tap, jazz, ballroom, ice dancing, modern ballet, and classical ballet. I have studied classical ballet and that is what I will be telling you about in this chapter. Classical ballet is different from all other kinds of dance, because it's based on five basic positions of the feet, because it's danced on the tips of the toes, and because it's danced to classical music.

Ballet had been the domain of royalty, of kings and their court. The word *ballet* is taken from the Italian word *ballare*, which means "to dance." Ballet was "invented" during the Renaissance in Italy, when Lorenzo de' Medici staged elaborate spectacles to amuse his guests. In 1700, ballet steps were made uniform when five basic foot positions were created by Pierre Beauchamps, who was dancing master to the French King Louis XIV. From that day to now, the five positions have not changed. Here is what the five positions look like.

First Position

With heels together, feet are turned out in a straight line. Beginners should turn the toes out at an angle of only 100 degrees. When you've studied ballet for a while and when your muscles are more conditioned, you can begin to approach the "ideal" first position of 180 degrees, shown below. Don't try for the ideal first position until you are ready!

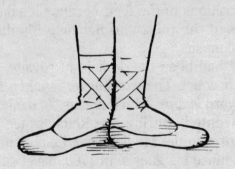

Second Position

Second position looks very much like first position, except that your heels are about one foot apart.

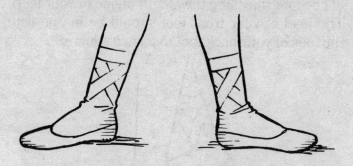

Third Position

As with first and second position, your feet are turned out with heels together, but in third position, one heel is touching the arch of your other foot.

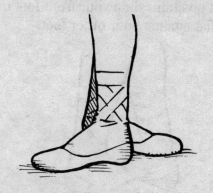

Fourth Position

Feet are turned out, with one foot placed in front of the other on a parallel line, separated by a distance of one foot (meaning the length of one of your feet)! The heel of your front foot should be in line with the toes of your back foot to form a square.

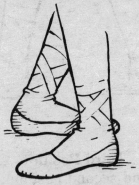

Fifth Position

From fourth position, slide your front foot until it is completely flat against your other foot.

The five positions can be executed with your right foot in front of your left or your left foot in front of your right. In all five positions the center of weight is equally distributed over your legs. Remember to keep your stomach in and to stand up straight. Keep your shoulders down and your arms rounded slightly, away from the body with your elbows lifted. The head should be centered, the neck free from tension, and the eyes focused straight ahead. The five positions should be done holding on to a barre for balance. The barre is literally a bar of wood fastened to a wall or freestanding in the ballet studio.

Although arm and head movements vary in ballet, feet positions do not. Whenever you see a ballet, you will know that the movements taking place onstage have come from one of the five positions.

There are also seven basic body movements in ballet: to bend (*plier*), stretch (*étendre*), lift (*relever*), jump or leap (*sauter*), dart or push (*élancer*), glide or slide (*glisser*), and turn (*tourner*). The names of the steps are all in French because the first national ballet school was in France.

You can walk into any ballet studio anywhere in the world and the class you'll see will be just about the same. First, warm-up exercises are executed at the barre. After all muscles are warmed up, the

Balance and strength are very important in ballet. Here, Darci and fellow students are warming up at the barre.

class continues in the center of the floor, where jumps and turns are executed. Everyone, from the very youngest students to prima ballerinas, take their classes the same way. Even members of the dance company take class in addition to practicing their roles on their own and rehearsing with the company.

Classical ballet is different from other forms of dance because the ballerina dances on pointe, on her toes, in special toe shoes. The shoes are covered in pink or white satin. The ballerina sews matching pink or white satin ribbons to the shoes and ties them around her ankle for support. It seems impossible, with such minimal support, that anyone could even stand in such a shoe. Even more incredibly, the ballet you are performing may demand that you hop, skip, or land on pointe. After years of study and the gradual strengthening of the foot, dancing on pointe does become possible and very enjoyable.

Putting on your pointe shoes is a lot like slipping your hands into a glove. You have a feeling of snugness and well-being. Tying the ribbons becomes a ritual, often repeated, that is very satisfying.

Pointe shoes are worn with tights, and the ballerina's outfit is complete with a short stiff skirt called a tutu. The tutu is usually worn very short, above the thigh so that the footwork of the dancer can be seen. It may be very decorative and beautiful, depending on the role. Some ballets may require different kinds of costumes, such as a long, flowing shift, instead.

Usually a ballerina also wears a headpiece of some sort. In classical ballets it is often a little crown, or a tiara. Tiaras are very elegant, handmade, and decorated with rhinestones. I always feel like a queen when a tiara is placed on my head.

Male dancers do not dance on pointe, and do not wear toe shoes. Instead, they wear soft leather ballet slippers, a tunic, and tights.

Classical ballet is further distinguished from other forms of dance because it is performed to classical music, usually symphonic music. A symphony is a piece of music for an orchestra divided into sections called movements. The acts of a ballet correspond to the movements of a symphony. For example, there is usually one movement in a symphony called the adagio. Adagio means "slow" in Italian. There is also usually an adagio section of a ballet and it is during this slow section that the pas de deux, the duet between a ballerina and her partner, is danced.

Modern ballet also relies on the five positions of the feet, but it is not always danced to classical music. It can use modern symphonic music, jazz, and other contemporary forms. Although it is usually danced on pointe, the movements in modern ballet are more varied than in classical, and less formal.

In any ballet, the prima ballerina dances the leading role with her partner, a male dancer, with an accompanying group of dancers around them, called the corps de ballet. Together they perform the steps and movements that the choreographer has created to give physical expression to the music. The music and the dance become one. As the choreographer George Balanchine once said, "See the music. Hear the dance."

By now you've probably guessed that ballet is about beauty, and that the ballerina, her partner, and the other dancers make beauty come to life. In the same way an artist creates a beautiful painting on canvas, ballet creates a living canvas onstage. When a ballet is in progress, with the swirling colors of the different costumes, I am reminded of a beautiful painting by the French artist Dégas. His paintings of ballets and of ballerinas are infused with life, with elegance, and with romance—just like a fairy tale.

Left: Darci at one and a half years of age. Below: Darci and her family.

CHAPTER 2

MY EARLY YEARS

My own tale began in Riverside, California, on June 4, 1964. I was born into a boisterous household of four brothers: Jackson, who is five years older than I am, then Harlan, Lindley, and Marty. We were all a year apart.

My father is a physician and when I was born, my mother was still teaching French and English in the local high school. With five of us, though, she decided to stay at home, except when she helped at my father's office.

Naturally, my mother found it extremely difficult to get baby-sitters for so many young children, and we were all taught to take care of each other. Our parents always treated us as if we were older than we really were. We were responsible for our actions. If we did something wrong, or if we were suspected of doing something wrong, punishment was swift. There was no discussion of whose fault it was—we all got it! My father is a perfectionist and we were expected to do well at whatever we did or try something else. We were not to waste our time or anybody else's. We learned to be practical and realistic about our abilities at an early age. We also learned to try our best and to be competitive in a very healthy way.

When my mother was not working, she made up for the time away from us by taking us to our favorite beach, Laguna Beach, or to our favorite place, the neighborhood pet store. We loved animals. We had a dog and a cat and more exotic pets such as iguanas, snakes, lizards, rabbits, and Iggy, our alligator.

One day Iggy got into our family swimming pool. He chomped through all the nets we used in trying to catch him. No one could go in the pool and our parents made us return him to the pet store. Secretly I was relieved because I had noticed Iggy hungrily eyeing our dog and cat.

Of our many pets, the snakes were the hardest for our parents to accept. We always managed to include them in our activities, much to our mother's dismay. A fairly large boa constrictor was loose in our house for about a week. Once Mom was dusting the furniture and discovered one of our pet snakes curled up snugly in a dried floral arrangement.

16

Believe it or not, Darci was once named Crash Kistler.

I always wanted to do whatever my brothers did. I guess you could say I was a tomboy. We built high, elaborate tree forts, played football and tennis, swam, water-skied and snow-skied, ice-skated, and rode motorcycles or ponies when we visited our grandparents' farm in Ohio. I was fearless.

All my brothers started riding motorcycles when I was five years old and were soon racing motocross (Honda 125s) and bringing home trophies. They proudly displayed them on shelves in our family room. I rode a motorcycle, too, and quickly earned the title "Crash Kistler." My brothers taught me to ride by putting me on a Honda Yamaha 80 and releasing the throttle. My first obstacle was a formidable one—a tree. Motorcycle riding was not at all scary, though. It was lots of fun.

My brothers joined a wrestling club as soon as they were old enough. Since they were very competitive and spent most of their time wrestling each other, they distinguished themselves right away. My brother Harlan won the first trophy in the family. This spurred my other brothers into action and soon our house was overflowing with trophies.

My brothers were dedicated to the sport and I watched in amazement as they worked out, ran, and watched their weight before competition. I learned a good lesson from them. I learned that you had to be tough and you had to work hard to get what you wanted. You also had to be unafraid to fail.

My brothers' hard work and dedication paid off as they won state championships, AAU (American Athletic Union) Awards, and even entered Olympic trials. Their dedication was to reward them with college scholarships when they were much older. They all placed in the NCAAs (National Council of Athletic Associations), and my youngest brother, Marty, won NCAA twice and was voted Outstanding Wrestler. They tell me that what they learned was discipline, inner strength, and the confidence to deal with any type of personality or situation they might encounter in life.

My parents didn't exactly want me to wrestle or race motocross, which made me really upset. How was I ever going to win my own trophy? I wondered. I remembered that from the time I was about three years old I had loved cutting out ballet pictures and coloring in my ballet coloring book and telling my mother I wanted do *that*. But all the ballet studios had told my mother I was too young and would lose interest if she enrolled me.

When I was five, a neighbor gave me a pink tutu to wear as a Halloween costume. And around that time my mother took us all to see a ballet performance of *The Sleeping Beauty* at the Hollywood Bowl. It was danced by England's greatest ballerina, Dame Margot Fonteyn, and Rudolf Nureyev, a Russian dancer who had danced with the Kirov Ballet until 1961. They were two of the best dancers of our time. My brothers thought it was extremely funny to see a man wearing tights, and they laughed during most of the performance. Not me! From the moment the two dancers came out onstage, I was in heaven, and from then on there was no stopping me.

In case my mother didn't get the idea that I wanted to take ballet, I started wearing my tutu around the house. Finally, she got the hint and

Darci striking a pose in her first tutu.

started me in a creative dance class. I enjoyed it because I had a wonderful teacher named Bonnie. But I did not really like modern dance. I wanted to dance on my toes. I wanted a real frilly tutu and all the feminine things that went along with ballet.

When I was six, the ballet teacher Mary Lynn Waterman allowed me to begin ballet classes at her studio in Riverside, which was called Mary

20

Lynn's Ballet Arts. From the moment I walked in, I knew I was in the right place. I loved ballet from the first class I took. I knew this was what I had been waiting for. I have often said ballet gave me purpose in life. It was all-consuming. I loved my classes, dreamed of ballet, and practiced on the slippery, tiled entry floor of our home, which proved disastrous many times.

I never wanted to miss a class. This sometimes annoyed my brothers and friends, especially when we were enjoying a day at the beach. I would make everyone rush to the car so we would make it home in time for class.

Mary Lynn, our teacher, was the perfect role model for a girl like me who loved everything that was beautiful. She was lovely and moved with such grace. We little girls were spellbound and wanted to be just like her. She instilled the love for ballet in all of us.

That year, in first grade, I took the clarinet in school. I started to learn about classical music. My mother would take me and my brothers to concerts at the Dorothy Chandler Pavilion and the Shrine Auditorium in Los Angeles.

My serious ballet study began when I was eight. I remembered my brothers' strenuous wrestling workouts. I thought I had to work out just as hard for ballet. My dad said that if we didn't sweat, we

Darci at nine, practicing at the Mary Lynn's Ballet Arts Studio.

weren't trying hard enough and wouldn't accomplish anything. As a result, I would sometimes practice to the point of hyperventilating. This was not good, and I soon learned to work hard but not too hard.

It still bothered me that I didn't have any trophies. My brothers seemed to have all the opportunities to compete. I didn't—or at least I thought I didn't. One day I noticed an ad in the *Riverside Press*, our local paper, announcing a Junior Miss beauty contest. All those who entered had to perform in some area of the arts. What caught my eye was the headline. Trophies were to be given!

I begged my mother to enter me in the contest and work the record player for me. Then I choreographed the dance that I was to perform. I included the most difficult steps I had ever heard of. My mother was horrified and thought I would never be able to do it. But she supported all the dreams of her children and didn't let me see how worried she was.

When we arrived at the competition, we saw there was no real stage to perform on, just a carpeted area. I actually wasn't upset because I didn't care at all about the beauty contest. I was just thrilled to finally have the chance to perform. I don't know how I made it through my dance on that carpet, but I've always felt that if I could do that I could do anything. And I won second place.

I proudly carried my trophy home and showed my brothers. They placed it with their trophies and teased me about it, telling me that I must have won it for my dancing and not my beauty. I didn't tell them that I had taken second place to a belly dancer!

About this time, my mother noticed an article in *Vogue* magazine. It was about a ballet school and company in New York City run by a man named George Balanchine. Mr. Balanchine had been born in Russia and had studied ballet in St. Petersburg at the Maryinsky Theatre Ballet Company, also known as the Imperial Ballet School. When the Soviet Union was formed in 1924, he and three other dancers left and became members of Diaghilev's Ballets Russes in Paris, where he soon became ballet master. In 1933 a writer and producer named Lincoln Kirstein convinced him to come to America to continue the tradition of the great Russian ballet. In 1934 the two men founded the School of American Ballet. The next year they formed the American Ballet Company, which was to become the New York City Ballet in 1948. The company fulfilled a dream for Lincoln Kirstein and fulfilled the greatest role of his life for George Balanchine.

The article also talked about how Mr. Balanchine would choose a certain perfume to match each dancer's personality. He knew each ballerina by her scent. If he stepped on an elevator that a ballerina had just been on, he knew who had been there. I had never heard of anything so exotic. I was enchanted.

The article included a photograph of Mr. Balanchine surrounded by a group of beautiful ballerinas. It was an overhead shot and he looked as if he were in a flower garden. I was completely enthralled by this article and spent hours reading and rereading it. I'm amazed it remained in one piece.

I continued to work hard and by the time I was eleven, I had been placed in the advanced ballet class. At that time, auditions were being held at the schools and in various parts of the country for summer scholarships to train with major ballet companies. My teacher was away, which was lucky, because technically you had to be twelve to participate, a fact my mother and I did not know. The entire advanced class—including me—was taken into Los Angeles to audition for the San Francisco Ballet, the American Ballet Theater and the magical company I had read about—the New York City Ballet, with its School of American Ballet.

At the auditions, there were teachers and representatives from each of the ballet companies. I wasn't sure what to expect. First, I was asked to lift my right and then my left leg to the front, the side, and the back, as high as I could. Then I was asked to point my left foot, then my right foot. I later learned that the teachers were looking for grace and style and natural ability as well as specific physical characteristics, such as a long neck, a good instep, good extension, and a well-proportioned figure. (Extension is the ability of a dancer to raise and hold a leg high in the air.)

My mother and I will never forget that day. It was her birthday and I desperately wanted to win a present for her. I auditioned for and was accepted by all the major companies! My mother said it was one of the best presents she had ever received.

When they found out I was only eleven, they told me I was too young. Then they learned that I would be twelve in June and decided it would be okay. Because of the *Vogue* article, I chose the School of American Ballet with no hesitation.

I couldn't wait for the regular school year to end and my summer ballet session to begin. When I arrived at the School of American Ballet (SAB), I was in for both a pleasant surprise and a big shock. The shock was that the training was much more advanced than what I was used to. I knew I would have to work very hard to keep up. I was not discouraged because this was what I wanted and the way I wanted to work. I was thirsty for knowledge and these teachers provided me with plenty to drink. All the teachers took their craft very seriously. I loved the whole experience: the adventure of being away from home, the classes, the teachers, absolutely everything.

The pleasant surprise was the realization that ballet classes are the same everywhere. The familiar details of the studio—the high ceilings, polished wood floors, mirrors lining one wall, and barre—were very comforting to me, especially since I was

Darci was comforted to see that ballet classrooms were similar in California and New York.

27

twelve years old and three thousand miles away from home.

Of course I was not there by myself. I had to have a chaperone. My mother and another mother split the time so they would not have to be away from their families for six whole weeks. I had never been away from home that long before. I really enjoyed writing letters during the first three weeks, but I started to miss my family. When my mother came for her three weeks, I felt much better. She took me sightseeing to the Statue of Liberty, the top of the Empire State Building, and all the other places I had read about. We also visited the Metropolitan Museum of Art and shopped at the big department stores. And finally we saw the Rockettes dance at Radio City Music Hall. It was quite a different style of dancing from what I was learning. We were taught a step called *grand batte-ment*, in which we kicked our legs very high, that would make us perfect candidates for Radio City Music Hall, where all the dancers stood in one long line across the stage and kicked their legs in unison. I decided that if I didn't make it as a classi-cal ballerina, I would try out for the Rockettes.

That summer I was asked to be in the movie *The Turning Point*. The movie is about a young woman studying to become a ballerina, an older woman who has given up ballet to raise a family, and a ballerina who is facing retirement. It features the ballet stars Leslie Browne and Mikhail Baryshnikov, as well as one of my teachers from the school, Mme Alexandra Danilova. It turned out that my scene was cut, something I learned when my family and I went to see the movie. We waited for my scene but it never appeared. I learned the hard way that the movie business can be tough. My cut didn't really matter to me, though, because it was a wonderful experience just being in the movie.

Each student was evaluated at the end of the summer. My evaluation went well, and I was invited back for the next summer. It was recommended that in the interim I study with one of the school's teachers, Irina Kosmovska, who often taught in Los Angeles. I had liked Irina's classes that summer so much that my mother and I decided to make the three-hour round trip from Riverside to Los Angeles each day.

Back home, I lived for Irina's classes. They became the focus of my whole life. Her classes were very difficult and prepared us well. Most important, they continued the training of the School of American Ballet.

My mother and I were to continue this routine for two years. My mother was also working in my dad's office and my brothers were involved in sports. It was a very busy time. I did my homework in the car. My mother never complained about the drive. She told me later that she cherished that time with me.

My brothers were pretty proud of me but they were still up to their old tricks. Sometimes I'd be doing my homework and they'd come in and flip me. Or else they'd sneak up on me while I was relaxing beside our pool and they'd throw me in. They were definitely annoying but I wouldn't have traded them for anything.

I eagerly counted the days until the next summer, when I would return to SAB. I knew that some of the students were to be invited to attend SAB all year and go to the Professional Children's School for academic classes. There were only 300 students in all the divisions of the school, with very few new students taken each year, so I knew there would be a lot of competition.

My school in Riverside, St. Catherine's, had been extremely understanding of my schedule, but I knew I wanted to study ballet in New York. I was about to start high school and I thought it would be a perfect time to leave. Why not get started as soon as possible, I figured. But even if I were asked to return full-time, I did not know how we could afford it. Living in New York was expensive. And my

Darci taking ballet classes at Irina's studio.

brothers would be starting college, one right after the other. I just hoped there would be a way.

At the end of my second summer session at SAB, when my mother joined me for the evaluation, the school said I had been awarded an Atlantic-Richfield Scholarship. I was the first recipient of this joint scholarship between the Atlantic-Richfield Foundation and SAB. It would pay my tuition and cover all my living expenses. Plus I'd be able to fly home twice during the year. It also meant that I would be leaving home at fourteen to live on my own in New York City.

My mother worried that I would miss the high school scene. When she had taken me to a football game during the previous school year, she had said, "Darci, you will be missing all this." There were cheerleaders and dance squads and flag routines and lots of excitement. I was so happy in my pursuit of dance that I told her immediately, "I don't mind." I knew I would miss my family and holidays and graduations and seeing my brothers win at big tournaments. But I knew what I had to do. I knew that to achieve a goal sacrifices had to be made. I had learned that from my brothers. As always, my parents left the decision to me. I decided to accept the scholarship and in September 1978, at the age of fourteen, I left for New York to pursue my dream of becoming a ballerina.

CHAPTER 3

ON MY OWN

People ask me how I could have left home at such a young age. I remind them that by then, at fourteen, I had already spent two summers in New York, and I knew I loved it. My life in New York felt like a video on fast forward. I could feel the energy from the city. I liked to work hard and I knew there would be plenty of that in New York for me. Besides, I had very little free time to think about being on my own.

My mom helped me settle in at the Swiss Town House, a dormitory-style place especially for the younger girls enrolled in both SAB and the Professional Children's School (PCS). There were also older girls already with companies such as the American Ballet Theater. My roommate was a girl named Barbara who was studying at the

34

Juilliard School of Music. There were even some friends from home, Teri and Niki, who were also studying at SAB.

And there was Lulu, my pet cockatoo. We weren't allowed to have a dog or a cat at the Swiss Town House, but we could have a bird. Lulu was a little bit

Darci and her favorite pet cockatoo, Lulu.

larger than what they may have expected. She was an umbrella cockatoo and about the size of a large chicken. Lulu would crawl into bed with me and loved to take showers.

I knew my parents were not worried about my living alone in New York. They knew that my schedule was so busy that, even if I wanted to, I couldn't get into any trouble. I just wouldn't have the time! My life was quite regimented between PCS for my academic classes and SAB for dance.

The daily schedule my first year was so jampacked with activity that I barely had time to breathe. I loved every minute of it!

PCS was a great school that adapted to the students' demands. Its enrollment included dancers and actors and all professional young adults and it went all the way through high school. The school was different from most schools because it revolved totally around our busy schedules. If we could not actually attend all our classes we were able to take them as correspondence classes. That meant we would do all the work on our own and then meet with our teachers once a week. We'd take the tests, of course, but we'd take them to fit into our schedules. Sometimes I'd take a test in the morning and sometimes I'd take a test after my afternoon ballet classes. Because of my crowded schedule, I took many classes on correspondence. Our curriculum was concise and well organized. We spent very few hours in school but we learned a lot.

Just as I was beginning my routine in New York, Niki, my girlfriend from home, decided to return to California to attend her regular high school and be with her family. I knew it would be easy for me to do that, too. I missed being teased by my four brothers and I missed all the fun that went along with the high school years. But I knew I had made the right decision. I had the full backing of my family. It was this complete support from my family that gave me the strength and courage to remain to study my craft and follow my dream. I wanted to work hard and be the best I could be at what I loved to do—dance!

Every day I would get up at eight A.M. and have breakfast downstairs with all the other residents. I would always feel sort of shy walking into the dining room and finding a place to sit. I felt as if everyone were watching me and that no one wanted to sit with me, because all of the girls were older and knew each other already. I knew the problem would resolve itself in time. A more immediate problem was getting accustomed to the food. Sometimes my mouth watered for a taco!

I would leave the Swiss Town House at eight

forty-five in order to be at PCS for my nine A.M. math class. I loved math. I've always found it so rewarding to find the right answer to a problem.

Math ended at ten A.M. and then I would rush, rush, rush, to SAB. Ballet technique class began at ten-thirty sharp. Usually the class would be with Madame Antonina Tumkovsky, who had been teaching at the school since 1949. When she was teaching, I always tried to arrive early. She gave a very demanding class with a very short barre. Mme Tumkovsky's barre was only a half hour long. So I would try to get there early and do my own warm-ups before class.

The other girls in the class were a little older and more advanced than I was, since I had just moved up from C1, the first level of the advanced division of the school, to C2. My technique was not as polished as a lot of the others, but I knew I would learn quickly in this class.

Next we would have a half hour of grands jetés, or big jumps, to work on our height and distance. Everyone in the class would sigh because this part was so strenuous. I wondered if my legs could take it. Yes! If this class didn't make my legs stronger, nothing would.

When class was over we would clap for Tumey, our pet name for Mme Tumkovsky. She worked us

Working at the barre helps to develop the strength to do the amazing steps we see onstage.

hard but her classes were always so challenging and built up our strength. The trick was to survive them.

We had other teachers for ballet technique. Suki Schorer's classes were intelligent and fast paced. Suki had been a ballerina with New York City Ballet and she knew exactly what we needed. She had a sharp eye and gave us good, practical corrections.

The classes we all awaited most eagerly and, in my case, the ones I lived for were taught by Stanley Williams. Stanley had studied and taught at the Royal Danish Ballet School. His classes were

Suki Schorer teaches her students to make their moves look effortless in her technique class.

unique. To observers watching us doing our small, perfectly executed movements, it may not have appeared as if we were working very hard at all. Within a few minutes, though, we would be drenched with perspiration. Stanley's classes were so complete that every muscle of our bodies would be exercised before the class was over. His was the ultimate ballet workout. To this day I feel that Stanley's training makes the dancers seem so light on stage that they look as if they are floating. Anyone who studies with Stanley approaches technical perfection.

Stanley's classes were so memorable that many of the dancers from NYCB would come back to SAB to study with him. Classes such as our Friday late class at five-thirty often had stars such as Peter Martins, Fernando Bujones, Mikhail Baryshnikov, and Gelsey Kirkland. I could hardly concentrate because I wanted to watch and learn so much.

Lyn Stanford played piano for Stanley's classes. Lyn's playing was so upbeat and witty that he brought out the best in us and made class fun. Near the end of class, when we were exhausted, he would play tunes we could recognize, such as "A Spoonful of Sugar Makes the Medicine Go Down," but with a ballet beat. The music made us forget our aching muscles and tired bodies. We left class feeling as if we had been to a party.

After the morning ballet classes, I would rush back to PCS for French class at twelve-thirty. My mother had taught French and made sure all of us kids studied it. My teacher at PCS, Mrs. Edlick, had lived in France and she told us lots of stories about what the country was like, which made class a lot of fun. I really enjoyed it, as my mom promised me I would.

After French class was over, I would race back to SAB for a three P.M. class taught by Andrei Kramarevsky. He was from Russia, where he had been a principal dancer with the famed Bolshoi Ballet Company. He had been at the school for only two years when I arrived there. I found him to be a very exciting teacher. His English was like my French: He knew only *un peu*. That means he knew a little bit! He actually knew only two words: *expensive* and *cheap*. If you made a mistake, he'd say you were cheap. If you did something right, you'd be expensive!

Mr. Kramarevsky taught the adagio class. In classical ballet, the adagio is the section danced by a male and female dancer in the pas de deux. In other words, in adagio class we learned to dance with a partner. The boys were taught how to lift and support the girls while we executed our turns. This was a very difficult class. The boys would hold us

Students at SAB learn to balance ballet and academic classes.

by our waist and lift us high into the air, sometimes standing still and sometimes walking across the floor with us up in the air. The boys would also hold us while we turned on pointe. It took a lot of timing and practice to get the teamwork right.

Adagio class was always a little difficult for me. I'd never really danced with a partner before, so I felt a bit awkward. The class made me feel the way I thought I would feel at my high school prom—

43

Darci and her classmates watch Andrei Kramarevsky teach the adagio class.

like a wallflower. There were only about twenty-five boys in the whole school, so each boy was in demand. Most of the boys wanted to dance just with the girls they liked or already knew, and Krammy, our pet name for Mr. Kramarevsky, never chose partners for us. As a result, I found the class very intimidating.

Even as an adult, this feeling of not being wanted or included, or of arriving at a party and not really feeling part of what's going on is still with me. It can be better explained in a ballet that George Balanchine choreographed, called *Serenade*. I would later dance this ballet, performing the Waltz Girl role. In the ballet, the Waltz Girl rushes in during the middle of a party scene, after everyone else onstage has stopped dancing. She conveys the feeling of being late and having missed something. She sees everyone else in his or her place and looks around for her own. Everyone acts as if she isn't there.

When finally she finds a place, all the girls start to walk offstage slowly. A man enters, weaving through the girls, and taps her on the shoulder. Then they do a beautiful waltz together. So she is the Waltz Girl.

The level C2 adagio class was at three P.M. on Fridays. Other afternoon ballet classes were toe, at three P.M. on Tuesdays, and variations, at two-thirty on Wednesdays and Thursdays, taught by Mme Alexandra Danilova. Variations are the solo parts in all the famous ballets. Mme Danilova taught us the roles just the way she had learned them in Russia. Mme Danilova had studied at the Imperial Ballet School in Russia at the same time as Mr. Balanchine and she left Russia with him in 1924 to join Serge Diaghilev's Ballets Russes in Paris.

At this time, she was frequently Mr. Balanchine's ballet partner. She became an international star throughout the 1930s, 1940s, and 1950s, when she danced with the Ballets Russes de Monte Carlo. Mme Danilova had been teaching at SAB since 1964. Her classes offered us a peek at where our instruction was taking us. Someday we would perform the roles we were learning. If we were really fortunate, we would perform them with the New York City Ballet.

We also took classes in music theory, structure, and notation, the recording of dance movement through symbols. When classes were finally over for the day, I would go back to the Swiss Town House and spend the rest of the day doing my homework, having dinner, and resting.

Darci at age 15 and her mentor, Mme Danilova.

I would usually take a ballet technique class at twelve-thirty on Saturdays and Sundays. Sometimes on weekends I would go to a museum or a concert or take a long walk with one of my friends. And for the classes I took on correspondence, I would have to do a week's worth of work on the weekend.

SAB was my focus and first love. Its graduates went on to be part of all the major ballet companies around the world, in San Francisco, Pennsylvania, Chicago, and all over Europe. But the school was primarily thought of as a training ground for the New York City Ballet. Being accepted into "the company"—the New York City Ballet—became the goal of everyone studying at SAB. Seeing the versatility of this great company, the dexterity of the dancers, and the degree of their accomplishment amazed us night after night. I thought we were taking class to be able to perform, but NYCB dancers could do so much more than that. They could play onstage. They hopped, skipped, jumped, ran, and were able to land on pointe—on their toes! In the slower ballets, they stretched their bodies to the music like human violin bows.

I loved my life and routine in New York, but as Christmas vacation approached, I became more and more excited. I couldn't wait to see my family. Harlan, Lindley, and Marty were in high school. My oldest brother, Jackson, was in college at UCLA. I wanted to hear all the stories about school and all about their wrestling tournaments.

I also couldn't wait to share the good news with my family that I had been chosen for two parts in SAB's annual Workshop performance.

The Workshop performance has always been an event eagerly awaited by people in New York and tickets are highly coveted. I was especially excited because I knew that most of the new members of the New York City Ballet were chosen from these performances.

As soon as we got back from our Christmas break, we started to rehearse for the Workshop performances, even though they were not until May. Stanley Williams had chosen me and Dagoberto Nieves to work with him on a new staging he had done of a pas de deux called *William Tell*, which was choreographed by the Danish choreographer August Bournonville.

Our rehearsals took the place of our regular afternoon classes. Once a week at two o'clock, Dago and I worked with Stanley on the *William Tell* pas de deux. Sometimes I would work with Stanley by myself. I loved rehearsing for Workshop with Stanley. A year later, Stanley said in an interview, "She caught my eye right away. It was her concentration, her capacity to work, her tremendous responsiveness to the tiniest clue. I could just look at her and she'd know what I meant. And when she danced, her whole body expressed the movement. Even her face was lighted with it. It's as if she was born just for that."

At that time I was also selected by Jean-Pierre Bonnefous, (who now spells his name Bonnefoux), a dancer with the New York City Ballet, to perform a ballet he was choreographing for the school called *Haydn Concerto*. Originally from the Paris Opera Ballet, he was a principal dancer with NYCB and married to Patricia McBride, another principal ballerina with NYCB.

Another amazing experience happened at the same time. Mr. Balanchine had choreographed a ballet in 1932 and 1944 called *Le Bourgeois Gentilhomme*, which he now decided to re-stage with choreographer Jerome Robbins for the New York City Opera. Jerome Robbins had danced with the company for many years and was at that time Ballet Master. *Le Bourgeois Gentilhomme* was a ballet (not an opera) based on the play by Moliere and with music by Richard Straus. The ballet was to star Rudolf Nureyev, Patricia McBride, Jean-Pierre Bonnefous, and dancers from SAB. He choreographed two parts for Darla Hoover and Stacy Caddell, two dancers in D class, the most advanced class. I was to be their understudy. I was to remain in the back of the rehearsals, learn their roles, and be able to step in if there was an emergency. It was quite exciting just to be in the same theater with all those famous people—especially

Mr. Balanchine, whom I had never actually met.

One day we were having a rehearsal in the main hall at the New York State Theater in Lincoln Center, (where NYCB performs), and Mr. Balanchine (or Mr. B., as everyone who worked with him called him) was sitting in the front of the room. Darla was leading her dance group across the main hall and I was practicing at the very back corner when, all of a sudden, I fell! It was not a graceful fall. It was a real crash. What an incredible noise I made. The music stopped and everyone in the room looked at me. I turned crimson and mumbled, "I'm sorry." Mr. B. looked over at me and smiled. Was I embarrassed! Many years later, I learned that Mr. Balanchine liked it when his dancers fell. To him it meant that they were dancing full out, which means they were dancing as if it were a real performance and not holding back. I wish I had understood his reaction then. It would have saved me much embarrassment.

Le Bourgeois Gentilhomme premiered at the New York State Theater on April 8, 1979. I did not dance in any of the performances but I loved the experience (fall and all) just the same. This was my first encounter with the opera world, and after that I would sneak into the theater and watch as many operas as I could. I met some of my favorite opera stars through a man named Charlie Wigler, who worked as a waiter in the coffee shop at the Empire Hotel across from the New York State Theater. Charlie knew everybody and everything happening in New York. Mom used to say he should have run for mayor. I loved Charlie immediately because he was such a character. He also loved the ballet.

I will never forget the first time I met Charlie. I was feeling very grown up, since I had just turned twelve and was on my own in the big city. I had just finished class and was dying of thirst. I ordered a Coke and then noticed others were asking for lemon in theirs. The restaurant was very busy but I managed to get Charlie's attention and I ordered a lemon in my Coke, too. The place was so crowded that Charlie threw it to me from across the room. I caught it and we have been friends ever since. Over the years I even graduated to catching a few plates.

May came sooner than I would have liked and suddenly it was time for the Workshop performance. I was to perform *William Tell* twice and the *Haydn Concerto* once. I was so nervous! My mom and dad flew in to see the performance. That morning they went with me to one of my favorite restaurants, called Bagel Nosh, on West Seventy-first Street and Broadway. For good luck I bought a little horoscope scroll for the day, but I knew I was just being superstitious. My mom put me at ease by telling me I would be beautiful. I was so happy she was there. I felt I was going to perform as a present for her, just as I had when I auditioned for my first summer session.

I made it through all my performances and in the August 1979 issue of *Dance* magazine, the dance critic, Tobi Tobias, wrote a review. "At this year's pair of Workshop Performances . . . the runaway hits of the show were the fifteen-year-old Darci Kistler and Dagoberto Nieves, who's sixteen, in Stanley Williams's staging of a pas de deux from Bournonville's *William Tell* . . . Kistler . . . is a real phenomenon." I was thrilled. It was a perfect ending to my wonderful, dizzying first year at SAB.

So that I wouldn't lose the momentum I had gained in school, I decided to remain in New York for the 1979 summer course. Soon after the Workshop performances, I heard that Robert (Ricky) Weiss, a principal dancer with NYCB, was choreographing a ballet for the thirty-fourth Caramoor Music Festival, held in a small town not far from New York City. It was a ballet to Ottorino Respighi's music called *The Birds*. I loved being invited to work in this ballet because it would be performing experience and also because of Lulu. Rehearsals were especially fun because Peter Martins and Kay Mazzo, two principal dancers with NYCB, were in the production and I could watch them up close.

The Birds premiered on June 16, 1979, in an open air theater, perfect for summertime. What I liked best about performing was the fact that, after hearing only piano accompaniment during rehearsals, the actual performance featured a full orchestra. After the performance, Peter Martins gave me his bouquet of flowers. I was so touched. I took them home and dried them and, to this day, I still have them.

Following the 1979 summer session at SAB, I went home to California. The time flew by. Our family was so excited to be together and do our usual adventurous things. We stayed at Lake Mohave and water-skied our hearts out, played tennis, swam all day long, and made numerous forays to Laguna Beach. My brothers and I basked in the sun and each other's company. It was a very precious time because our busy schedules rarely allowed us all to be in the same place at once.

I found it a bit difficult just to rest and not dance but with our local ballet studio closed for vacation, my mother and I had to go into Los Angeles again for classes. I was much easier on my mom that vacation and I told her we would only have to go in every other day! I took classes at Stanley Holden or at the Lichine Ballet School with Tania Lichine.

Darci at home in California 'performing' her chores.

As time passed and I realized I hadn't been working as much as I was used to, I began to worry about falling behind in my technique. And as my vacation came to an end, I found myself holding on to every moment and appreciating all the details of our home life: the smell of food as my mom was in the kitchen preparing dinner; the sunsets, which in New York are not as visible or spectacular as on the West Coast; sitting on our green lawn dreaming of the future; waking up to the sound of voices and knowing how much I would miss the routine and companionship of my family.

Suddenly, I felt scared and anxious about leaving. I began to doubt myself and wondered if I was good enough to make it in New York.

As I boarded the plane, though, a sense of peace came over me and I knew that everything would be okay. I would try my best and if it was not my destiny to be a ballerina, God would take care of me. I comforted myself with the thought that I could always go back home to my family.

CHAPTER 4

MY SECOND YEAR

My second year at SAB started out much the same as the first year, but it was soon to bring more and more exciting changes in my life. The school kept me in the C2 level. I continued to enjoy my academic classes. My favorites were history, math, and science. I loved their precision. If I hadn't been studying to be a dancer, I know I would have wanted to become an astronaut.

I stayed at the Swiss Town House again with my same roommate, Barbara. Lulu was back with us again, too, in a new role in my life. She was going to teach me how to act like a bird.

For our Workshop performance my second year, Mme Danilova wanted us to do the second act of *Swan Lake*. She had Mr. B. observe her variation class to choose who would play the lead, Odette. He chose me to dance the role! The role called for me to play a swan (Odette) who turns into a woman (Odile) and back into a swan again. It was actually Lulu who taught me how to flutter my arms like a bird. I hoped she would also teach me how to fly, but for some reason she never did!

I was very excited to have been selected but I was also very apprehensive. I had just seen the Russian ballerina, Natalia Makarova—perhaps the best Odette ever—perform the role and I could not imagine myself repeating the same role in front of people. I was just a beginner. There is so much drama and pathos in this ballet that it requires a great deal of maturity from its ballerinas. It is not a part for a fifteen-year-old! Classical ballets are the most difficult to perform, because the standards are very high and the public is familiar with the ballets. If a dancer makes a mistake, the audience will usually notice it. This particular classical ballet has been danced for over one hundred years, so many in the audience know it extremely well.

I was an adventuress, though, and my excitement soon overcame my doubts. I dreamed of nothing else but *Swan Lake*. Freddie Franklin, a dance partner of Mme Danilova and a great dancer, helped her stage the Workshop performance. Mr. B. was very busy working with the company and was not able to

Darci dancing the role of Odette the swan at a dress rehearsal of the Swan Lake Workshop performance.

help, but he said he would come to our last rehearsal onstage to offer last-minute corrections.

Mr. Balanchine had a tremendous influence on his dancers. One day I had an experience that I can only describe as amazing. I was late getting to SAB because I had to meet with my French teacher. I ran to the school and rushed down the hallway to the dressing room. Usually the hallways buzzed with noise and excitement but on that day it was so quiet! I knew something important was about to happen.

I dressed quickly and went to class. Suki Schorer was teaching. I heard some of the girls say Mr. B. would be observing class. I knew it was Mr. B.'s presence I had felt in the hallway. I shall never forget it.

Mr. B. watched our class and at the end he picked a few girls to be apprentices for the New York City Ballet. I was one of them! We would not really be part of the company but we would get to perform with them onstage. Labor and union regulations required that we could only perform in three ballets per season.

From this point on in the fall of 1979, things happened in fast forward. I had had no real warning or preparation for the life I was about to begin. It was going to be sink or swim and I was going to have to figure out a lot of things on my own. At first I was intimidated by the thought of finding a place to dress in the huge corps dressing rooms on the fourth floor of the New York State Theater. There was no curtain and the female dancers all got dressed in one big area. I also had to learn to put on my own stage makeup. False eyelashes proved the most challenging and they still do. At first it would take an hour to put on my makeup. Now, years later, it takes only fifteen minutes. Putting on makeup is probably what I like least about performing.

One of the other new dancers, Stacey Caddell, and I stuck together and helped each other. We watched everyone to see what they were doing. Another dancer named Vicki Hall showed me how to sew my ribbons on my toe shoes. Everyone was very helpful.

Everything was new to me. It was now up to me to call the rehearsal tape. That meant I would have to call a special phone number and listen to prerecorded information that told us who would be rehearsing each day and when our rehearsals were scheduled. I would also have to see Roland, the man in charge of all the dancers' shoes—both female and male.

Dancers are always changing the specifications and sizes of their toe shoes. As an apprentice, I did not have my shoes custom-made for me, but dancers in the company shared shoes with us that they did not need. This was a real help to us apprentices financially. Each shoe is different and made by a different maker, so borrowing shoes provided us with a rare opportunity to see which maker fit us best.

Most of the ballerinas' shoes are from Freeds of London or Capezio. The male dancers' shoes are from all different companies. Our company budget for shoes is $600,000 annually. That may seem like a lot of money, but it's not. Toe shoes are very fragile and each pair lasts for only one performance, so we go through an enormous number. They are the most important part of our costume. I knew that when I became part of the company, I would get to choose the type of shoe I wanted and which maker I wanted. To me, it would be better than winning the lottery!

During my first season, the apprentices danced in all the performances of Balanchine's *Symphony in C* with music by Georges Bizet. My dance was in the fourth movement, which is very fast. I was so nervous I wanted to go even faster. I had to hold myself back. During the second movement, the adagio section, I would stand in the wings, entranced. It was usually danced by Suzanne Farrell, partnered by either Sean Lavery, Adam Luders, or Peter Martins. It was so beautiful and moving, it seemed to embody my picture of ideal love.

I also danced in Balanchine's *Firebird*, with music by Stravinsky and decor by the wonderful Russian artist Marc Chagall. *Firebird* had been the first great success of the New York City Ballet, when it was performed at the City Center for the Performing Arts in New York, starring Maria Tallchief, a ballerina who had been married to Mr. Balanchine. The ballet is based on a Russian fairy tale and tells the story of a prince who captures a bird while hunting one day. The bird is the Firebird. She gives him a feather to win her freedom. In exchange, she will come whenever he needs her. It turns out that the prince does need the Firebird to escape from the evil sorcerer Kostchei, who has a spell over the princess he loves. She brings him a sword. I danced the role of one of Kostchei's monsters. It was fun being a monster because I got to run around onstage in ballet slippers, without having to worry about steps. We were all reprimanded, though, for having too much fun and laughing onstage.

The apprentices were also called to dance in *The Nutcracker*. This ballet is the reason why apprentices are selected in the fall. *The Nutcracker* is performed during the whole month of December and it is very demanding on the dancers. Corps members dance two roles every performance plus matinees on Saturday and Sunday. It was extremely difficult for me. I had to take extra good care of myself that month so that I could keep up the pace.

The Nutcracker is based on a story by E. T. A. Hoffman about a girl named Marie who receives a Nutcracker doll at a Christmas party. That night Marie dreams that her toy soldiers come alive and fight a band of huge, ferocious mice. The Nutcracker heroically fights the three-headed Mouse King, but is about to be overcome when Marie throws her shoe at the king, and he runs away. Then the Nutcracker becomes a prince and takes Marie through the land of the Snowflakes to see the Sugar Plum Fairy.

I was chosen to dance in a few different sections: the Spanish scene and the Snow scene, my favorite. By January 1980, I had performed thirty-nine *Nutcracker*s!

On New Year's Eve, a lot of the dancers tried to do something funny during the performance. I say "tried" because Mr. B. and Ronnie Bates, the stage manager, told them not to. Some people got past Mr. B. and Ronnie by changing the choreography onstage! Some of the girls wore leg warmers, mittens, and hats in the Snow scene. Others came out onstage with sunglasses, party favors, and horns, as if they were going to a New Year's Eve party. I felt people were paying to see a real performance, so I behaved myself, but I had to admit the evening was very funny. I did dance as well and as big as I could and for that reason, I started the New Year off with a real bang!

My mom had come to see me dance with the company. I was so excited to have her here, I tried to dance extra exuberantly. I came out onstage in the biggest grand jeté, or leap, I could manage— only to land on my backside! The artificial snow had made the stage slippery. It happened so fast I didn't have time to think. As I was sliding across the stage, I heard the music and managed to get up and hit my ending pose exactly as the last note sounded. I was totally embarrassed at the time, but my fall has made for many laughs since. My mom and I could hardly eat our dinner that night because we were laughing so hard.

Long after *The Nutcracker* performances were over I still found snow in my dance bag and in my room at the Swiss Town House. I figured I would probably get rid of the last bits of snow just about the time *The Nutcracker* rolled around again the next year.

During my apprenticeship with the company, I took class as usual at the school every day unless Mr. B. taught class for the company. I was lucky because my very first class with the company was taught by Mr. B. We started with pliés in first position, and then I moved into second position. Mr. B. slapped me on the backside and stopped the class! He asked me where I was taught how to do second position like that. I said, "At your school, Mr. B., the School of American Ballet." Then he said, "Well dear, now I shall teach you how to dance!" From that day on, Mr. B. did exactly that, either by telling me things directly or by teaching me things through his ballets.

While I had my new responsibility to the company, I still had my responsibility to SAB. Mme Danilova worked with me once a week on *Swan Lake* for the Workshop performance. I loved the music and I felt enveloped by it when I danced it. It was a wonderful experience working with her on this great role. She was passing on to me what she had learned dancing with Serge Diaghilev's Ballets Russes. She made me look at Odette—half woman, half swan—from the womanly side and not as a moving swan. This made sense to me. I didn't want to pretend I was a swan or pretend I was anything else for that matter. I just wanted to move as beautifully as the music.

One day during the spring of 1980, Rosemary Dunleavy, the ballet mistress for the New York City Ballet, came to watch a rehearsal. Rosemary

Backstage, Darci adjusts her toe shoes for the dress rehearsal of Swan Lake.

is in charge of the dancers and the ballets for the company. She assigns roles to the dancers and helps them rehearse their roles. She also helps select the new members of the company. And that's why she was there that day. The next day, a few other apprentices and I were told we were now officially in the company—just like that. I was told by Rosemary in the hallway near the drinking fountain. I will never pass that drinking fountain again without remembering that moment! Nothing would change, really, except that now I would make money for doing what I loved, and I could dance in more than three ballets each season. I would have to get a social security card and sign a contract, and my schedule of ballets and rehearsals would now increase rapidly. And, of course, now I would officially have my own toe shoe maker, someone at the factory in England who would actually make all my shoes!

I still had the Workshop to prepare for. Mr. B. came to our stage rehearsals and was very nice to me and provided some very helpful corrections. For the seven P.M. Workshop performance on May 12, 1980, I stood in the wings with my partner, Cornel Crabtree. As I listened to the overture I said a little prayer that I would dance my very best. I loved dancing *Swan Lake* so much, and the music sounded so grand that it transformed me and took away all my nervousness. It was a beautiful day, one I shall always remember. My mother and father had flown to New York. Afterward, my mother gave me one dozen white, long-stemmed roses. I had always collected glass unicorns and now I began to collect swans.

I got even more valuable performing experience thanks to Jacques D'Amboise, who at the time was principal dancer with NYCB. He provided me the opportunity to dance with his son, Chris, at Madison Square Garden for their annual benefit for the National Dance Institute. Jacques has done so much for New York schoolchildren by introducing them to the world of dance. The D'Amboises are a wonderfully talented family and I enjoyed meeting all of them.

I finished my tenth grade at PCS and was eager to learn more about NYCB and to perform in more ballets. SAB was soon to begin its summer session but I was not going to be part of it. I was going to Saratoga, New York, for three weeks, to perform with the company during the summer season.

I felt sad to be leaving the School of American Ballet. I knew I would always be able to return to take classes, but I felt the same way I had felt when I left home two years earlier. It was like leaving my second family. It felt as if I were starting all over again as the last person in the very back row. But I also felt I had nothing to lose and everything to gain. I could only move forward.

In Saratoga I stayed at the campus housing at Skidmore College. I roomed with four other young new dancers with the company. At first, we all stuck together like glue, but slowly we began to branch out and make different friends.

I loved Saratoga. The theater was outdoors and open on three sides. It was like performing in a magic glen. When I returned to New York, I moved out of the Swiss Town House and into my own apartment. My mom came to New York to help me and Lulu move in.

As I got settled in my apartment, I grew accustomed to my new life as a dancer for the largest dance company in America and one of the greatest ballet companies in the world. My dream had finally come true.

CHAPTER 5

WORKING WITH MR. B.

Much has been written about Mr. Balanchine's genius as a choreographer, but I knew him as a real person, and that is how I like to remember him. He entertained people with stories about his youth in Russia. He was very witty and did great imitations. He always looked out for his dancers. I knew he cared, even if it was the simple gesture of adjusting my headpiece before a performance.

Soon after I moved into my apartment, we left again to go on tour in Europe. I had never been out of the United States. One day in Paris, after a long rehearsal, we took a break for lunch. I wasn't really sure what to do, so I walked into the first restaurant I saw. I realized immediately it was much too expensive for my budget. The waiters noticed that my attire was not appropriate so they turned me away.

Mr. B. demonstrating a dance step.

To add to my embarrassment, I saw Mr. Balanchine with a group of important people across the room. At the same time, he noticed me. I think he realized that I was too embarrassed to walk out of the restaurant and he immediately asked me to join them for lunch.

While we were all engaged in conversation, we noticed a butter dish, but no one could figure out how to open it. I gave it a try and soon had it apart and back together again, like a puzzle. Mr. Balanchine was delighted! He made me feel very special.

That trip to Europe was my first experience with extended travel. Dancing in the historic theaters of Europe made me see how the history of ballet really tied in with European history. Visiting the many beautiful museums overflowing with art treasures began a fascination with art that I still have. Walking the European streets surrounded by a wealth of romantic architecture made me feel as if I were in a living museum. I took in everything I could.

During our European tour and back in New York, when I was not scheduled to dance, I would watch as many performances and dancers as I could. There were so many ballets to see and so much technique to learn. One day, Mr Balanchine had me sit on a chair with my back to the stage. "Don't watch," he said. "Just listen to the music."

That was Mr. Balanchine's genius. He reduced everything to its simplest and most essential element. He always told us why we were doing things, rather than just telling us what to do. Thus, he taught us how to think. Everything that I have read and learned since has told me that what he said was true: Ballet is not *accompanied* by music. It *is* music. Balanchine never used too many steps in his ballets; the movements always seemed to fit the music perfectly. My body was never sore or tense after performing a work he had choreographed. I always felt that it was functioning the way it should, the way it was trained, like a finely tuned instrument being played. After a performance, I always experienced a sense of exhilaration and then fullfillment.

Mr. Balanchine also taught me that if I listened to the music, such as Tchaikovsky's music to *Sleeping Beauty*, I wouldn't need to look elsewhere for inspiration. The music would move me and make me react in a certain way. Even in a story ballet, I wouldn't have to feel as if I were acting. I'm sure Mr. Balanchine wanted me to feel, not act, so there would be no barriers between the dancing and the audience. That is the mark of a great dancer.

Mr. Balanchine was very witty and had a great sense of humor. I had always wanted to introduce him to my mother because he was such a great man. My mother always said, "No, to him I'll just be a ballet mother. His association is with you, his dancer." One day, my mother and grandmother were visiting New York and we met Mr. Balanchine on the street. I thought this was the perfect time to introduce them, with three generations present. He smiled and nodded and then turned to my grandmother Mrs. Russell Kinner, and said with his charming accent, "And you are ze mudder, right?" We all laughed and of course, it made my grandmother's day!

He also talked a lot about God, the Bible, and going to church during his youth in Russia. He had a beautiful outlook on life, I think, because he had a good soul. He never thought of himself as a great choreographer but rather as a craftsman. He said he never invented. God had already invented; he assembled. He quoted the Sufi poet, Rumi, when he said "Whosoever knoweth the power of the dance, dwelleth in God."

The first year that I was in the company, Mr. Balanchine spent lots of time with me. He saw how much I loved to dance, and he began casting me to do major roles. He would always say, "I don't have much time," because he knew he was getting old. I was sixteen and he was seventy-six. With Mr. B. in the wings, I didn't feel nervous dancing on stage. He entrusted me with some of the choicest roles in the repertoire, including the Swan Queen role in *Swan Lake*.

This was the same role I had learned from Mme Danilova for my Workshop performance only five months before. But this occasion was to be different. I was going to dance this role at the opening of the Washington, D.C. season at the John F. Kennedy Center for the Performing Arts.

I will always remember the night of October 8, 1980, as the most thrilling—and terrifying—night of my life. As I stood backstage at the Kennedy Center Opera House, my heart began to pound. My parents were in the audience and I thought that if I could see them, I'd feel more assured. I peered around the stage curtain but could see only total darkness. It was eerily quiet. The only indication that an audience was there was an occasional cough or rustle of a program.

I bent down to adjust the ribbons on my toe shoes, and the familiar movement made me feel more secure. The moments just before I step out onstage can be wonderful, but also agonizing.

I saw Mr. Balanchine standing in the wings of the theater and remembered what he had told me. "Don't act. Just be in the moment. Be yourself." He took away every inhibition, every fear I had with two words. "Don't act."

The stage lights dimmed to the color of moonlight, and I heard the most hauntingly beautiful music in the world. My head cleared and my limbs felt lighter than air. It was as if I were being held aloft by helium balloons. I glanced over to Mr. Balanchine, who stood motionless in the wings. He gave a slight nod, and I knew at that moment that I would be fine. My body glided out onstage. The music soared and enveloped my very being.

> *"The excellence of her training showed in every move she made, the carriage of her head, her body placement, the melodiousness of her steps. All the rest—and it's the rest that mainly stamps her as a dancer of awesome artistic promise—is her own: the natural musicality, the instinctive plastic fluency, the absolute self-possession (in the face of inevitable nervousness). . . and expressive projection."*
> —Washington Post

Dancers are not supposed to dance for their reviews, but the *Washington Post* review that appeared the next day made me feel much better. I'll explain why.

On opening night, I ran out onstage early, probably because I was nervous or too eager. My poor partner, Sean Lavery, entered. He was not supposed to be able to see me, and there I was already out onstage. It was a terrible moment! Finally, after what seemed to be an eternity, Sean stepped over to me and took my hand. I rose off the floor and we danced our pas de deux. I was in tears over my mistake, but thank goodness for one very kind *Washington Post* critic—who didn't point out what was wrong.

I danced all four of the *Swan Lake* performances that week and was heartened by the reviews because they all spoke about my improvement. Sali Ann Kriegsman in the magazine *Ballet News* said, "Her dancing is ample, assured and joyous. If she is to be Balanchine's next muse, we have much to look forward to."

The best review, however, came from my father. In an article about me in the *Washington Post*, he said, "She was always good. She's always been serious about what she wanted to do. I don't know much about dancing, but I get goose bumps when I watch her. I hate it when she leaves the stage." That vote of confidence from my dad was better than any review I could ever receive!

In 1980, her first year in the company, Darci performs
Swan Lake *with Sean Lavery.*

During the first week of the 1980–81 Winter season in New York, I danced principal roles in four works and made nine debuts. I also performed the coveted adagio role in *Symphony in C* and both the Dew Drop and Sugar Plum Fairy roles in *The Nutcracker*. One of those performances was very special. It was the first time I danced with Peter Martins. We danced in *The Nutcracker* on January 4, 1981. Our performance went very well.

My first season with the company was filled with lots of magic moments like this. Toni Bentley, a good friend of mine, captured perfectly what it was like to be in the company and especially to work with Mr. B. in her book, *Winter Season: A Dancer's Journal*. It is a treasure of a book, as she observed and poignantly recorded the 1980–1981 season.

Even though I was performing a number of principal roles, I was still technically in the corps. I cannot explain how wonderful it was to be dancing these great roles with this great company. Life certainly did seem like a fairy tale. Clive Barnes, who was then the dance critic for the *New York Post,* wrote that it would be a time like no other in my life, and he was right. Mme Danilova said, "There is perfume in her dancing that makes you think, 'how beautiful.'"

What a lift! I did have some bad moments, too. In November 1980, while doing my debut in *Symphony in C,* my costume started to unravel at the side seam. I remember thinking that even if it fell off, I had to keep dancing. One of the magazines captured the moment and you can see clearly that disaster was waiting in the wings!

Another time disaster actually struck, when the glue from my false eyelashes stuck my lashes together during a performance, making it impossible for me to see. I had to feel my way around onstage until my next exit. What an incredible sight I must have been to my poor partner! And I learned the hard way about waterproof mascara—after a disastrous performance in the corps in Saratoga Springs. My perspiration made my mascara run down my face. It looked like I was crying. It took me a while to realize that I had to use waterproof mascara.

Because of my youth and seeming ease in dancing leading roles, magazines such as *Time, Newsweek, Vogue,* and *People* called me a "baby ballerina." There was a lot of publicity. Mr. Balanchine knew that publicity could prove distracting, so he did not permit many interviews. I did not care about any of that; I just kept on dancing. Besides, I knew that in

Peter Martins helps Darci practice one of her moves.

1933 the Ballets Russes had three ballerinas who were each fourteen years old. I knew that no matter how good I got, someone better would always come along. So I kept my feet firmly planted on the ground and my focus on dance.

I danced more and more. My roles increased to include just about everything in the regular repertory.

In addition to the ballets of George Balanchine, I also danced many roles from Jerome Robbins ballets. His ballets are vivacious and naturally beautiful. The Peter Martins ballets I was in were beautifully contemporary, incorporating an inherent keen, clear, intelligence.

Soon after, in May of 1981, I was promoted to soloist. "She takes to the spotlight like a plant in the sun," wrote the critic Tobi Tobias on September 21, 1981, in *New York* magazine. I continued to get wonderful roles, to push myself, and to learn from Mr. Balanchine.

And I continued to receive compliments for my dancing. The late Rudolf Nureyev, in an interview with the *New York Times* in December of 1981 asked, "Have you seen that new one—seventeen years old—Darci Kistler with the New York City Ballet? Such aggression in her legs, such attack . . .

There are four other ballerinas on stage and she's the one you're looking at . . . There's that devil inside." I didn't have any devil in me! I just loved to dance. At the end of the spring 1982 season, I was made a principal dancer.

CHAPTER 6

MY INJURY

Until this point my story had been very much like a real fairy tale. Life was good. I was accomplishing goals I had set for myself in dance and was privileged to be dancing major roles. Then things changed. In November 1982, Mr. Balanchine became ill and died on April 30, 1983. I felt a tremendous sense of loss. Everyone felt helpless, and didn't quite know what to do. Peter Martins and Jerome Robbins were made co-directors, and they maintained the performance schedule. Dancing onstage, without Mr. Balanchine standing in the wings, I knew that this was the best tribute that could be given him. To this day, I always feel him there when dancing his ballets and I know that, in this way, he never really dies.

Darci and Peter Martins in a 1981 performance of
The Magic Flute.

At Balanchine's funeral, Lincoln Kirstein gave a beautiful eulogy. "Grief becomes mere self-indulgence. Gratitude and joy must be our feeling for what he gave us, and determination that his work and ideals be honored and preserved and used to illuminate the future for ballet." These words of wisdom helped me immensely to accept his death.

A mysterious incident occurred the day Mr. Balanchine died. When I returned to my apartment, I noticed a bumblebee there. When I awoke the following morning, it was dead right on my pillow, next to my head. I preserved it in a crystal box.

Just as fairy tales have an ogre or misfortune in them, so did ogres start to appear in my life. Shortly before Balanchine's death, I was rehearsing for a television special of the ballet *The Magic Flute* and slipped on a piece of tape on the studio floor. I experienced tremendous pain in my right ankle and could not put weight on it. There was so much swelling that an X ray did not reveal much and I continued to try to dance. Finally the pain was unbearable and I had to stop.

I was very discouraged. My foot wouldn't heal, yet no one seemed to know what to do about it. At first the problem was diagnosed as a sprain. When the pain did not go away with time and I had difficulty walking, we knew it was more than a sprain, so the company sent me to England for surgery. A doctor skilled in balletic surgery was called in from Denmark. He was a very skilled doctor who had been recommended by Dr. William Hamilton, NYCB's orthopedic consultant. The problem was that he did not speak English and I did not speak Danish. I showed him the X rays and pointed to the injured area. He operated in a local clinic for forty-five minutes. It was excruciatingly painful, but he did remove the bone chip from my ankle bone that seemed to be what was causing me so much trouble.

I returned to the States on crutches and began physical therapy with Marika Molnar, NYCB's athletic trainer. I also took classes slowly, thinking everything would be all right and I would be back onstage again soon. Instead, my ankle got worse. It had a huge, purple bump that would not go away. The pain was still there and I had to discontinue therapy and all classes. After going through surgery and experiencing no benefits, I was very afraid my career was over. I was devastated and needed the comfort of my parents and my home, so I left for California.

Unfortunately, my parents were living through the ogres of their own fairy tale. They were in the middle of getting a divorce. It was such a bleak time. My mother and I were both very sad. Yet we were able to console each other and help each other through our grief.

My mother learned of a place called the Southwestern Orthopedic Group at Centinela Hospital in Los Angeles while watching a football game on TV. She heard that they had successfully operated on some of the major sports stars. She figured if it worked for them, it could work for me.

We met Dr. Yocum there. He said that there was a possiblity that the bone chip had splintered and I would need a second operation. However, he did not want to operate too soon. He told my mother that if this operation did not succeed, there would be no alternative but to cut the nerve in my foot. This would make it impossible to dance, because I would not be able to feel the floor.

So I went through six months of physical therapy, with no ballet at all. I couldn't even put weight on my foot. After six months, I had the second operation. I stayed in California to recuperate. While I had a cast on, I would sit for hours in front of a big mirror in our entry hall and listen to ballet music and move my arms. This allowed me to devote time to work on my arm movements.

I returned to New York, completely out of shape. My teacher, Stanley Williams, was wonderful to me and worked with me patiently every day for a whole year. Once again, I underwent physical therapy with Marika Molnar. I had to begin literally from the beginning. When I could finally do a full workout at the barre, I started to resemble my old self again and wanted to perform.

I really didn't think my foot was ready, but I was tired of watching from the sidelines. There were times it hurt too much even to go near the theater. The doctor had informed me that bone injuries usually require five years to heal completely. Well, I just couldn't wait five years.

I first did *Afternoon of a Faun*, a beautiful ballet with choreography by Jerome Robbins, that is not as demanding physically as it is emotionally. I performed it first at the evening performance on February 9, 1985, with Afshin Mofid as my partner. We had danced in this ballet together three years earlier, and I was comfortable dancing with him. It felt wonderful to be back onstage. The critic Clive Barnes wrote in the *New York Post*, "Welcome back, welcome home, Darci Kistler." I thought that was so very special. It confirmed to me again that New York is a human city. I had wanted to dance my very best to thank the company and the New York patrons for all their support. I was incredibly encouraged by Jerome

Darci's mother Alicia Kistler was a great comfort to Darci during her long recovery period.

Robbins's reaction: "Darci's dancing today is a continuum of all that she promised before."

I was next cast for *Swan Lake* as my major reentry to ballet. My mother had flown in to see the performance and to be there for me. It was a very anxious night, because I wanted to do so well. Rumors were flying that I wouldn't be able to dance as well as before because my foot wasn't strong after the two years off. I wanted to put those rumors to rest. Plus, I was overcome with emotion about going onstage again.

The performance started well, but just as I was beginning to feel confident and was in center stage, there was a jabbing pain in my foot. It was as if the hunter in the ballet had shot me in the foot with his crossbow. I took a real swan dive and felt the wind knocked out of me; I hit my chin, my stomach, and my elbow. Later Mother said I still managed to keep my feet pointed upward behind me! There was a loud gasp from the audience.

After what seemed an eternity but was only a few seconds, I jumped to my feet and continued the performance. My mother claims that any time I've fallen in a performance, I've always managed to regain my composure and give even more. I hoped that would be true tonight. *Swan Lake* is a ballet with a lot of arm movements, and I realized

92

that everyone could see my elbow swelling larger and larger until, finally, the performance ended. I realized sadly that my comeback was not meant to be, at least not yet.

More time off and months of therapy followed. It was very upsetting because in my mind I kept hearing Dr. Yocum telling me that the nerve might have to be cut. It was a disheartening time, too. I would attempt to do a role when my foot felt better and then with no warning, I'd have to take time off because it would be so sore. Understandably, critics and fans misunderstood and speculated about whether I really wanted to dance. And in low periods, I admit, I asked myself that question, too.

A guardian angel must have been watching over me, because with time and therapy and patience my foot slowly began to heal. I finally reached the point where I was considered to be back and could also withstand the rehearsal and performance schedule.

It was now 1987, just about five years from the date when I first injured myself. My long recovery period did hold one very nice surprise. Artists always hear that audiences are fickle and that someone is here today and gone tomorrow. The reverse happened to me. People would stop me on the street and inquire how I was. It was so nice to know they cared. I think it gave me a deeper sense of commitment when I realized how much ballet meant to all these people. It also made me even more eager to return to the stage.

Something else kept me going, too. Two women named Anne Belle and Deborah Dickson made a wonderfully poignant movie called *Dancing for Mr. B: Six Balanchine Ballerinas*. It consisted of one-on-one interviews with six ballerinas with whom Balanchine had worked closely, accompanied by film clips of each one. Each ballerina discussed her relationship with Mr. B. and what he meant to them. "He was like a painter or a gardener," I said. "He loved to see things blossom." I realized that I had come to be one of those "flowers" surrounding Mr. Balanchine in the *Vogue* magazine article that had first inspired me. Being part of the movie kept me in touch with ballet during the time I wasn't able to perform.

I finally regained my strength and confidence through my work with Stanley Williams. David Howard, of David Howard's Ballet School in New York, is another excellent teacher who was a great help with his strengthening classes and his morale building. With their help I was able to return to my complete repertoire. And I was ready for the challenge of my life.

CHAPTER 7

THE ROAD BACK

As I was recovering, I heard some news that made me want to conquer my injury completely and get back onstage. There was much publicity about a new staging of the ballet *Sleeping Beauty*. I knew Mr. Balanchine had planned to do this ballet, but he died before his dream could be fulfilled. Peter Martins, our director, would take up the challenge. I thought it would be a wonderful tribute to Mr. Balanchine. The story of *Sleeping Beauty*, by Charles Perrault, had always been one of my favorite ballets and I wanted more than anything to dance the leading role of Aurora. Her whole life is enacted onstage—her birth and christening, when the wicked witch puts her under an evil spell; her sixteenth birthday, when she pricks her finger and falls asleep for a hundred years; and finally her maturity, when she is awakened by a kiss from Prince Désiré. It is a tender story and contains some of the most beautiful music ever written, by Tchaikovsky, accompanied by some of the most difficult dancing.

In the early stages of my recovery, it was unrealistic for me even to consider this role. I was injured, my foot was weak, I was out of shape. I had to fight the doubt and uncertainty of whether I would regain my strength and performing ability or would need that final career-ending operation. I lived one day at a time, with *Sleeping Beauty* always on my mind. Constancy of purpose and the joy of my work—however slowly I had to take it—became my allies through this difficult time.

To complicate matters, a series of other injuries plagued me as well. The most serious of these was a strain of polio virus that lodged in my left shoulder blade, making it impossible for me to raise my left arm. More time had to be given up, making my goal of dancing *Sleeping Beauty* even more unobtainable.

Instead of fighting my body and making demands on it, as I had always done before, I slowly learned to listen to it, allowing it to dictate to me. I had to learn to pace myself and listen to my body. If my foot became too sore, I wouldn't push it.

Slowly I started to make progress. My immediate

Darci had to practice twice as hard after her injury.
Here she is taking a break with fellow dancer Ib
Anderson.

goal was just to be able to take group classes. My future goal, of course, was to perform *Sleeping Beauty.*

Many days I felt it was childish to harbor a belief in dreams. I told myself it was only reality that counted, and the reality was that I could not dance. I attended therapy and after many months gradually worked my way back into the dance studio.

I shall never forget how wonderful it felt to be able to use my body again on the first day back in class. Some people probably regard ballet class as just fatigue and perspiration. It makes me feel as if my body is functioning as a totality. Each part is worked until the whole body becomes completely drained, then cleansed and finally refreshed, made new again. Class is such a wonderful experience, something I always look forward to.

Throughout this time, SAB students wrote me encouraging notes, as did ballet fans. My teachers were very patient and supportive. My mother and brothers bolstered my spirits with long telephone conversations. My brothers had all sustained severe injuries to knees and shoulders through wrestling, so we compared injuries and therapies. This really helped me to maintain good spirits and it kept me working.

Around this time, I received a nice honor. I was one of the recipients of the 1990 *New York Woman* magazine award. It was special because my mother made the presentation to me. In her introduction she told everyone what I was like growing up, how I cut out pictures of ballerinas when I was three, how I began my training. She told the funny story of how I managed to get a trophy for myself. She covered everything. She ended by saying, "I wish to thank *New York Woman* magazine again for this honor bestowed on my daughter, Darci, and to thank God for this special blessing, this special daughter. I love you, Darci."

My days were filled with more hard work. Finally I was cast again in *Afternoon of a Faun* for my return to the stage after my disastrous *Swan Lake.* Understandably, I was very nervous. I had not performed onstage for a long time. My only consolation was that my foot felt more healed than it had for my last return.

When the music started and I removed myself from all the worrying and just concentrated on the music and dance, everything was fine and I lost my nervousness. I realized that if I could just stop thinking about myself, I could shift my focus to my job.

The next role to challenge me on my return to the stage was performing *La Sonnambula* with Ib Anderson and Robert La Fosse, two wonderful dancers. Mme Danilova had created this role and

Darci and Jock Soto in a performance of Afternoon of a Faun.

Allegra Kent, a great ballerina, had made her name in it a few years before. It is always difficult to perform a ballet that another dancer has been closely associated with. However, the beauty of this art form is that a role is preserved by being passed on and danced again by another dancer.

Allegra generously helped me learn the role. I've always considered it an honor for a retired ballerina to teach a younger one. It reminds me of passing the torch at the Olympics. Someday, I will proudly do the same. When people ask me how I will feel when I can no longer dance, I will tell them that, just as my talent was given to me, someday it will be passed on to someone else.

La Sonnambula is an eerily beautiful piece in which an innocent poet is killed. The ballerina in the title role is sleepwalking and senses his death. Prior to his death, the poet chances to behold her sleepwalking in the garden and dances a hauntingly beautiful, but also playful pas de deux with her. This ballet is very mysterious and spellbinding. I loved performing it. My mother attributed my affinity for it to my habit of sleepwalking as a child! The music, lighting, and setting of this ballet enhance the ominous air of mystery.

There were periods when the strain of daily performances took their toll, and my foot required additional time off. My frequent absences were difficult for fans and critics to understand, as once they saw me back onstage, they questioned why I danced so seldom. It was difficult for me to understand as well. When my foot felt ready, it seemed the choreographers were afraid to use me, in case I couldn't perform. I am sure that they knew how much I wanted to perform and always respected how hard I worked. Then an interesting thing happened that left no doubt I was really back.

During the Jerome Robbins Festival, which ran from June 5 to June 17, 1990, my foot was fine and I was able to perform throughout the festival. It was glorious to come through when needed. It was also very satisfying and made me extremely happy because Jerry had choreographed on me when I was beginning my career.

After the festival, all doubt seemed to disappear about my return. As a result of so much dancing all at once, my foot did suffer a slight relapse. It was another exasperating period, as plans were in progress for *Sleeping Beauty*. Even though it was the most difficult thing to do, I stayed off my foot.

I got a lot of support, too, from the dance community. First, I was featured on the cover of the February 1991 issue of *Dance* magazine, with an interview inside. It was a wonderful feeling to grace the magazine that had been my constant companion for so long. It was also startling to see myself on the cover after admiring so many other dancers in the past.

The reason I maintain my belief in dreams is that my foot did heal, and I was able to start working again, just about the time plans were formalized for *Sleeping Beauty* and casting was being done. I felt that it might still possible to do this exquisite ballet for which I felt such a rapport. Imagine my happiness when the casting sheet was put up and I was scheduled to dance opening night, April 25, 1991!

The role of Aurora in *Sleeping Beauty* is one of the most difficult roles in all of ballet to dance. There's one section where the ballerina is required to balance on one toe, with both arms and one leg extended, for a full few seconds. I'm happy to say that I was able to do it every time. The reviews complimented Peter Martins's choreography and my dancing. Arlene Croce wrote in *The New Yorker*, "Kistler was as fragrant, as tender, as poignant as one could have wished, not just a storybook character come to life but a real human being struck down by fate."

It was an incredible experience to perform the first ballet I had ever seen, my inspiration to "do that" as my mother recalls. Well, I did "do that" and have never regretted it.

An interesting thing happened when I knew for certain I was dancing *Sleeping Beauty*. My mother sent me a congratulatory card with this message, "Now your prince will come." Well, she was right. Eight months later, during Christmas week of 1991, Peter Martins and I were married.

Darci and Peter Martins.

Performing Sleeping Beauty *was a dream come true for Darci.*

CHAPTER 8

MY LIFE TODAY

Since my comeback, I have been very lucky. I have taken extra-good care of my ankle and I have not been injured. I was invited to the White House under the Reagan administration. My performance to honor Mme Danilova at the Kennedy Center Honors took place during the Bush administration. And on May 6, 1991, I was one of the recipients of the Capezio Dance Award.

Another award that meant a lot to me was the American Academy of Achievement's Golden Plate Award. Held each year in a different part of the country, the awards ceremony brings together outstanding students from high schools nationwide to meet outstanding individuals from various fields.

The purpose is to give young people the opportunity to meet the honorees as real people and find out how they achieved their goals in life.

I was fortunate to be one of the honorees at the thirtieth annual Golden Plate awards banquet, on June 29, 1991, in New York City. Oprah Winfrey presented the award and Peter, the recipient for dance the year before, introduced me to the audience. He spoke so well! I was touched by his tribute.

When it came time for me to accept the award, I was very nervous. Dance training did not prepare me to make speeches. I had written some notes but I knew I wouldn't be able to look at them. I decided to forget the notes and wing it. Here are a few things I said.

"You have all heard the phrase 'I'd rather be dancing.' Well, that's never been more true than now! I'd like to thank you for honoring me, but even more so, for including me among such distinguished members.

"The other recipients of this award have all spoken about the importance of believing in yourself and recognizing what you wish to accomplish. I recognized at eight years of age what I wished to become. I accepted and respected my talent, and through belief in myself and perseverance, I brought my life to fruition.

"I was also very lucky to have good teachers and one very wonderful mentor. They taught me so much. Perhaps the most important lesson they taught me is to find my own worth. It's important to learn from someone but it's important to make it on your own. I pass that lesson on to all of you. Don't try to be anyone else but you. In order to reach your goal, don't be afraid to fail. Good luck to you and God bless you all."

What is my life like today? Peter and I live in New York City in an apartment not far from Lincoln Center for the Performing Arts, the home of both the New York State Theater and the School of American Ballet. The New York City Ballet performances, rehearsals, and our company classes are at the New York State Theater.

I am sad to say that Lulu died in 1982. She was actually quite old, twenty-five, when she died, and I think she had a good life. I have another cockatoo now named Eagle. We also have two dogs: a very frisky and large six-month-old golden retriever puppy named Lex, so named because we got him at a pet store on Lexington Avenue in New York City, and a female golden retriever named Mocha.

My routine is pretty much the same every day. I get up around nine A.M. and I walk our dogs. Then I read the paper. I like to linger at home in the morning, because I know that sometimes I won't get back until eleven o'clock at night. Class is at ten-thirty and it ends at noon. Rehearsal usually lasts from noon until three P.M. Then we get an hour off and we rehearse again from four until six, or seven if there are a lot of roles to rehearse. There were lots of roles to rehearse for last year's spring season in May and June 1993. It marked the tenth anniversary of Mr. Balanchine's death. We presented seventy-three of his ballets. It was an especially grueling season but it was also uplifting.

When rehearsals are over, then it's time to put our makeup on. The performances begin at eight P.M. My days are so busy that I barely have time to eat. Some days I'll have a bagel for breakfast and something from the health food store for lunch. Sometimes I'll have a cup of tea or some chicken soup before a performance to give me strength.

The interesting thing about ballet is that dancers are always practicing, always taking class, always learning. As Mme Danilova says, "Getting to the top is quite easy. Staying there can be very slippery. A lot of young dancers think that once you are there you don't you don't have to work. But just the opposite is true."

I continue to learn other things, too. In the last few years, I have learned to scuba-dive and to play the piano. I love to read biographies, poetry, and

Darci has many other interests besides dancing, like playing the piano.

science fiction. And I love to travel. In 1985 I went to Africa with two of my friends.

My whole family still lives in California and I talk to them very often on the phone. And my four older brothers are all still very close.

My fairy tale continues. Last spring, I was one of the three recipients of the 1992 *Dance* Magazine Award, "for distinguished careers in dance," as the magazine describes it. The award was presented to

Darci is still very close with her four brothers. From left to right: Marty, Darci, Lindley, Harlan, and Jackson.

me on April 13, 1992, by Mme Danilova. I hope she and I will continue to exchange tributes for a very long time to come!

Last summer, the New York City Ballet filmed a movie version of *The Nutcracker*. Unlike my first experience with *The Turning Point*, this time my part stayed in. I danced the role of the Sugar Plum Fairy. The movie stars everyone from the New York City Ballet, and features Macaulay Culkin as the prince. It's actually the same role he had danced onstage with the New York City Ballet when he attended SAB. The movie's premiere was Christmas 1993.

I think a lot about my future. I hope my ankle will stay strong. The 1988–89 season was my first full season without an injury. But I know things can't stay that way. I danced a lot of the 1990 spring season in pain, and I couldn't dance in all the performances I wanted to.

I still love dance. Even when my body aches all over or I've been rehearsing all day and performing at night and don't get home until eleven P.M., I still want to get up the next day and start all over again. I know I can't be a ballerina forever. I've always tried to remain interested in other things. I'm interested in veterinary medicine, for example. But I think that when I'm older, I'd like to teach very young dancers—from six up to the ages of twelve or thirteen. I've learned so much from my teachers that I'd like to pass that knowledge along. And since I grew up in such a happy family, I'd like to have a child someday.

CHAPTER 9

A FINAL WORD

Over the years, as I became more and more focused on my goal to be a ballerina, I found myself reading biographies of great men and women. I always hoped to find out how they achieved their goals. I also found that biographies offered tremendous insight about life in general. The British statesman Disraeli wrote "Success in life is the result of constancy of purpose." I interpreted this to mean that I must apply myself to what I like and I must put in the required hard work to achieve my goal. And that's what you must do.

If you decide to investigate the world of ballet for yourself, try to find the very best ballet school in your area. Always go with the best training. This can be said for any career you want to pursue. It will eliminate the need to "unlearn" what you might learn incorrectly. You will also avoid injuries that could occur from improper training, and this will save you a lot of time.

If a large ballet company is in your area, it will usually offer a school for young dancers.

I happened to attend an audition in Los Angeles for summer training and my life was changed forever. It is always good to inquire where and when auditions for such programs will be held. The listings in the back of *Dance* magazine provide an excellent source. The School of American Ballet holds auditions all around the country every year.

It is good to attend ballet performances whenever you can. Seeing dancers execute steps with grace and finesse makes the daily repetition of ballet classes uplifting and instills in you an eagerness to attend that next day's class! It's important to see there is an end to the means and all that work is for a purpose.

It is also good to read as much as you can about dance. When I was a little girl, I would await the arrival of *Dance* magazine every month. It's good to read reviews to see what the experts look for during a performance. Reviews can be found in many non-dance magazines, too, such as *New York* magazine and *The New Yorker* as well as all the major newspapers in the country.

Darci dancing.

During early adolescence, girls can experience a feeling of emptiness in their lives. You may not be old enough to work part-time, and it can be boring to hang out at the malls or watch a lot of TV. Boys generally have a number of athletic programs from which to choose. Ballet training can often fill that void, benefit the body, and give an incredible sense of purpose.

Ballet study provides students with an edge, a keener awareness of life. Combinations of steps that form a dance routine can be extensive and complicated, forcing you to listen carefully, follow directions, and concentrate.

The greatest benefit of ballet is the enhancement of the soul. Dancing to the most beautiful music in the world deepens the soul and cannot help but make you a better person. Dance is a celebration of the world of music. You become aware of classical music, the purest form of music, when, previously, you may never have been exposed to it. You are introduced to composers and famous dancers and read about the trials they overcame in their own lives.

What you learn in ballet are skills that will be utilized thoughout any endeavor in life, and the sooner acquired, the better. Teachers point out that many dancers learn more readily in school. I feel it can be attributed to the fact that they are focused at an earlier age and are used to listening and following directions. Having a purpose in life is a wonderful thing.

Ballet is an exquisite art form that offers limitless possibilities. It can give you a life, a great life. I know it did for me. When I was injured, I thought I'd never dance again. Through perseverance, hard work, and lots of prayers, I was able to fulfill my dream and dance the role of Aurora in *Sleeping Beauty*. It was the first ballet I had ever seen when I was a little girl and it has been the highlight of my career so far.

Yes, dreams do come true. I hope my life has convinced you of that and has inspired you to find your own dream. You may be asking yourself, "Well, it worked for her, but will it work for me? She just had a propensity for ballet." That's the beauty of dreams: everyone has their own. You just have to find yours, then believe in it enough to make it happen. I ask you to have the foresight to dream, and I beg you to have the courage to follow your dreams.

Selected Bibliography

If you can't find some of these books in your bookstore, you will probably be able to find them at the library.

Books for Young Readers

Berger, Gilda. *Magic Slippers: Stories from the Ballet.* Illustrated by Vera Rosenberry. New York: Doubleday, 1990.

Craig, Janet. *What's It Like To Be a Ballet Dancer.* Illustrated by Barbara Todd. Mahwah, New Jersey: Troll Associates, 1989.

Diamond, Donna. *Swan Lake.* Illustrated by the author. With an introduction by Clive Barnes. New York: Holiday House, 1980.

Dufort, Antony. *Ballet Steps: Practice To Performance.* New York: Clarkson N. Potter, 1985.

Fonteyn, Margot. *Swan Lake.* San Diego: Harcourt Brace Jovanovich, 1988.

Goodall, John S. *John S. Goodall's Theatre: The Sleeping Beauty.* New York: Atheneum, 1980.

Gross, Ruth Belov. *If You Were a Ballet Dancer.* New York: The Dial Press, 1980.

Isadora, Rachel. *Opening Night*. New York: Greenwillow Books, 1980.

Krementz, Jill. *A Very Young Dancer*. New York: Alfred A. Knopf, 1976.

Rosenberg, Jane. *Dance Me a Story: Twelve Tales from the Classic Ballets*. New York: Thames and Hudson, 1989.

Streatfeild, Noel. *Ballet Shoes*. Harmondsworth, England: Penguin, 1976.

Verdy, Violette. *Of Swans, Sugarplums, and Satin Slippers: Ballet Stories for Children*. Illustrated by Marcia Brown. New York: Scholastic, 1991.

Adult Books

Balanchine, George. *Choreography By George Balanchine: A Catalog of Works*.

Bentley, Toni. *Winter Season: A Dancer's Journal*. New York: Random House, 1982.

Dunning, Jennifer. *"But First a School": The First Fifty Years of the School of American Ballet*. New York: Viking, 1985.

Kirstein, Lincoln. *Thirty Years: Lincoln Kirstein's New York City Ballet*. New York: Alfred A. Knopf, 1978.

Lawson, Joan. *The Principles of Classical Dance*. With photographs of Anthony Dowell by Anthony Crickman. New York: Alfred A. Knopf, 1980.

Martins, Peter, with Robert Cornfield. *Far From Denmark*. Boston: Little, Brown and Company, 1982.

Reynolds, Nancy. *Repertory in Review*. New York: The Dial Press, 1977.

Taper, Bernard. *Balanchine: A Biography*. New York: Times Books, 1984.

Tracy, Robert, with Sharon de Lano. *Balanchine's Ballerinas*. New York: Simon and Schuster, 1983.

Ballet Magazines

Dance magazine. Published monthly.

Dance Pages. Published quarterly.

On Pointe: The Magazine for Young Dance Enthusiasts. Published quarterly.

Ballet Movies

DANCING FOR MR. B.: Six Balanchine Ballerinas. Produced by Anne Belle, with Martha Parker, Associate Producer. Directed by Anne Belle and Deborah Dickson. PBS Great Performances. Featuring interviews with Mary Ellen Moylan,

Maria Tallchief, Melissa Hayden, Allegra Kent, Merrill Ashley, and Darci Kistler. 87 minutes. 1989.

GEORGE BALANCHINE'S THE NUTCRACKER. Performed by the New York City Ballet with children from School of American Ballet. Produced by Robert A. Krasnow and Robert Hurwitz. Arnon Milchan, Executive Producer. Directed by Emile Ardolino. With Darci Kistler, Damian Woetzel, Kyra Nichols, Bart Robinson Cook, Macaulay Culkin, and Jessica Lynn Cohen. Minutes not available. 1993.

THE RED SHOES. Presented by J. Arthur Rank. Written, produced, and directed by Michael Powell and Emeric Pressburger for The Archers. Screenplay by Emeric Pressburger. With Moira Shearer, Léonide Massine, Robert Helpmann, Anton Walbrook, Marius Goring and Ludmilla Tcherina. 136 minutes. 1948.

THE TURNING POINT. A Herbert Ross film presented by Twentieth Century-Fox. Distributed by CBS/Fox. Written by Arthur Laurents. Produced by Herbert Ross and Arthur Laurents. Starring Ann Bancroft, Shirley MacLaine, Mikhail Baryshnikov, Leslie Browne, and Alexandra Danilova. 119 minutes. 1977.

About the Authors

DARCI KISTLER is one of the principal dancers in the New York City Ballet. She moved from Riverside, California to New York City at the age of fourteen to train with the School of American Ballet, and was accepted into the New York City Ballet when she was sixteen. She resides in New York City with her husband, Peter Martins.

ALICIA KISTLER, Darci's mother, graduated from Ohio State University with a degree in French and English. After teaching high school French and English for a number of years, she resigned to raise her five children. Today she lives in Riverside, California, where she is working in real estate.